"*Millennials' and Generation Z Guide to Voting* impressively consolidates the complexities of voting into an accessible and readable format, offering readers the opportunity to gain insight into specific areas of the voting process. With many individuals increasingly asking the question of "Why?" when it comes to voting, Levine and Wisdom do a masterful job in illustrating the rich history behind it and the related facets that influence it. In a time when politics is in a constant state of flux, making it difficult for younger and newer voters to ascertain how their votes fit into the larger puzzle, this resource serves a guiding light. A political science student myself, I see this as an immensely valuable tool.

**—Noah Kurzenhauser**
Political Science B.A. Student
Portland, Oregon

Voting is a right and a privilege. We only get the opportunity to make a difference if we choose to participate. This book was so helpful to understanding voting — and how one person can truly make a difference!

**—Jacqlyn Burnett**
Los Angeles, California

To be honest, I never paid attention to why it was important to vote, as I thought it didn't really impact me. Boy, was I wrong! 2020 alone has proven just how important it is to get out and vote. When it comes down to deciding who to vote for and where you stand, it can be very overwhelming. *Millennials' and Generation Z Guide to Voting* helped me work through my misunderstandings when it came down to getting the politics actually involved in voting. This is a book that is SO important and NEEDED in this decade. It helps map out a clear idea on why you need to vote and how to do so effectively. This is something every young voter needs!

**—Cassandra Blake**
Millennial and parent of Generation Alpha (Future Voter)
Tampa, Florida

*Millennials' and Generation Z Guide to Voting* is a fantastic resource for understanding the intricacies of the U.S. political process.

**—Walt Dawson, PhD**
Portland, Oregon

As a Millennial and a voter, I have been dismayed that my fellow Millennials are not always enthusiastic about voting. *Millennials' and Generation Z Guide to Voting* provides a stellar response: all the information to counter common excuses about not voting, plus a whole lot of support for how to choose candidates, what to expect, and how to contribute. Read this book and get out the vote!

**—Jennifer Felner, PhD**
Postdoctoral Scholar
San Diego State University, California

As a Millennial, I am deeply concerned about the prospect of a government that does not embody or prioritize the values of my generation. The *Millennials' and Generation Z Guide to Voting* addresses these concerns, providing the context to make informed decisions. This user-friendly guide synthesizes all I need to know in order to optimize my ability to contribute, through my vote.

**—Sarah Holland, MSW, MPH**
Portland, Oregon

# MILLENNIALS' & GENERATION Z
# GUIDE TO VOTING

# MILLENNIALS' & GENERATION Z
# GUIDE TO VOTING

What No One Ever Told You
about the Importance of Voting

JEREMY LEVINE
JENNIFER P. WISDOM

Published by Winding Pathway Books

WINDING PATHWAY BOOKS

ISBN (print): 978-1-7330977-2-7

ISBN (e-book): 978-1-7330977-5-8

Book design by: Deana Riddle at Bookstarter and
Jerry Dorris at AuthorSupport.com

Cover design by Diego G. Diaz

Photo credit: Diego G. Diaz

For more information or bulk orders, visit: www.leadwithwisdom.com

Printed in the United States of America

# TABLE OF CONTENTS

# FOREWORD

I entered adulthood at a time of unrest. I was 18 years old when the financial crash of 2008 hit, leaving my generation in similar economic uncertainty as Generation Z finds themselves in today with the effects of the COVID-19 pandemic.

But the ties that bind us as Millennials and Zoomers run deeper than the economies we've come of age into. We are the first digital natives: folks who grew up in a world where our experiences were not limited by our physical space, but instead expanded by technology.

We have big dreams and high expectations. We challenge the question of "what's always been" for "what could be." At the same time, we suffer from a slew of issues prevalent among us, most unique to our generations: unattainable home ownership, crippling student loan debt, racial injustice, climate change, gun violence, rising housing costs, and income stagnation.

With problems as large and looming as these, it's hard to feel like our singular votes can make a difference. Perhaps most frustratingly, it can often feel that our politicians are out of touch with our opinions. And that's because they are.

Regardless of which political side of the aisle you're on, there's a stark contrast between the people and the politicians. In one example, according to a Pew Research study, 49% of Millennial & Gen-Z Republicans believe the government is doing too little to reduce the effects of climate change (vs. 25% of older Republicans.) Yet a Republican Senate and Administration is instead reversing more than 100 environmental protections of previous administrations.

This, unfortunately, should be no surprise. In this book, Jeremy Levine and Jennifer Wisdom outline the ways in which money, and specifically corporations and their interests, influence elections. You mix this outsized influence of money with reliable, high propensity to vote generations like Baby Boomers and the Silent Generation, and you have a perfect storm for overshadowing the voices of a younger generation.

It seems an impossible scenario to solve: How do we get these politicians to listen? The reality is actually quite simple. Every politician, whether they're in your party or not, whether you support them or vehemently disagree with them, is fighting for your vote. Or, in some cases as Jeremy Levine and Jennifer Wisdom outline in this guide, they are fighting for you NOT to vote. In either scenario, you and I — the voters — have the power. Not them. And in large numbers, our voices and power grows.

The Millennial Congresswoman, Alexandria Ocasio-Cortez, rose to fame after unseating a 20-year incumbent, running on issues core to the Millennial and Gen-Z voting block. AOC warned supporters ahead of her election: "This race is winnable, and don't let anybody tell you any different. Because the power out there, I'm telling you, is an illusion."

The more we consistently turn out to vote in every election, the more weight we carry in reliably influencing elections, and the more our politicians will be forced to meet our demands or be voted out in favor of someone who will.

Millennials and Zoomers are set to make up 37% of the electorate in 2020 (compare this with Baby Boomers at 28%.) Yet we don't vote at nearly the same rates as generations above us. If we did, we'd have a greater influence on elections, based on the sheer number of us.

But for our generations, voting is about more than just who we put in office. We have the opportunity to not just elect, but to push our politicians and our parties to create and support a platform that meets the demands of our generations and our changing world.

Millennials and Zoomers, as so many young people of generations prior at the forefront of change movements ask: If you have power, what is that doing for us now? And when we don't get those answers, we show up with tools for change — we protest, as we've seen in overwhelming numbers due to the racial justice movement prominent in 2020. We use social media to fundraise and power grassroots organizations and campaign. We run for office. **And we vote.**

Each of these tools is necessary. Each one amplifies the message we send to those in power. Each one must exist alongside the other. Millennials and Zoomers have the opportunity to drastically change the political landscape by voting alongside major movements, harnessing the collective power of grassroots coalition building, and promoting the youth-driven organizations behind them.

One example of this is the recent re-election of incumbent Senator Ed Markey from Massachusetts. Markey, a 74-year-old white man, could not look further from Millennials and Zoomers, who will be the most racially diverse generations to date. Yet his championing of climate change action in co-authoring the Green New Deal alongside AOC earned him the support of the youth-driven climate activist group the Sunrise Movement. So when Markey was being challenged by a young Kennedy for his seat, Sunrise mobilized their youth for Markey. Senator Markey put Zoomers at the helm of his operation — organizing digitally amidst a pandemic to a victory of 10+ points. This was the first time a Kennedy has been defeated in Massachusetts. After his win, Markey tweeted "Thank you, zoomers."

In these races, turnout plays a huge role. But turnout does more than just win elections. It sends a message for our demands. Winning in a landslide large margin vs. a small victory means something to politicians and to the future of our political landscape. This is another way the tool of voting amplifies our message, alongside the other tools at our disposal.

We have the platform and the numbers to win elections. Do we have the will to vote? Do we have the belief that our vote can drive meaningful change?

The politicians of generations past are frightened of us. They are frightened of our demands and of our voting power. Will we be brave enough to believe in this power we have? If we are, it means we need to show up in every election, every year, and vote for every office. If our vote wasn't worth anything, they wouldn't be trying to stop us from voting.

In this guide, Jeremy Levine and Jennifer Wisdom provide a wealth of knowledge for Millennials and Zoomers to become informed, consistent, and confident voters in every election. Between learning about how our electoral systems actually work, the history of our political parties, and what exactly a state legislator actually does, this book will help to empower a new generation of voters to drive the change we wish to see in the world.

Rosalia Cefalu
Volunteer Organizer

# HOW TO USE THIS BOOK

**M**illennials' Guides books are not necessarily best read cover to cover. We encourage you to review the Table of Contents and identify something that looks interesting to you about voting. Turn to those pages to start learning!

Each topic includes a brief description and some ideas you may want to consider. These ideas may be historical context for why voting is so important, information about who is trying to control voting (and voters!) in the U.S., or how to see through "fake news" to understand what really matters for your vote. Most importantly, each of the chapters emphasizes the importance of being an active citizen:

◆ Learning about your community, state, or country, possibly for the first time

◆ Conducting your own research to understand issues and individuals up for a vote; and

◆ Casting your ballot so that your voice can be included.

As you work through this information about voting in the U.S., you might get frustrated. You might feel like this is information you don't need to know or that it doesn't affect you. You might think that politicians do not care about what you think or how you feel about particular issues. Part of being a citizen in a democracy, however, is to take part in voting. No matter how much you choose to pay attention to and participate in the democratic process, the democratic process will always impact your life and place in society. You do not need to be an expert on every issue or be an expert about every facet of our democracy, but to not educate yourself enough to understand how your vote can make a difference and why voting is important, when there are people around the world fighting for the very same right to vote, is an exceptional form of privilege.

Each of you reading this book is a unique person with ideas, opinions, and feelings to share with the world. Our hope is that this book can make it easier for you to do so. Good luck voting!

## PART 1

# Your Vote Matters

# CHAPTER 1

---

# Do You Know Why Your Vote Matters?

We get it. Voting may seem like a hassle, and how much does one vote even matter anyway? But if voting didn't matter, people wouldn't try so hard to restrict it. Moneyed groups that have an interest in the outcome of the election try to restrict voting in all kinds of ways. They enact these roadblocks because voting matters. Every vote matters, every voter matters, and *every vote counts*. Here's why.

1. **Voting is a right of citizens in a democracy.** Many people around the world don't have the right to vote in a democratic election. As citizens in a democracy, it is our right to vote, just as it is our right to peaceably assemble, have reasonable privacy, and live our lives without undue government influence.

2. **Elections have consequences.** You have opinions on health insurance, gay rights, abortion, civil rights, and climate change. Voting lets you support your own agenda for what you think the country should look like.

3. **It's important to make your voice heard.** You may think that as a Millennial or member of Generation Z, it's hard to make your voice heard. Well, here's your chance! If all people in these two generations vote, that will be about 100 million voters – nearly a third of the U.S.! There are now about as many Millennials as there are Baby Boomers eligible to vote, which makes Millennial

+ Generation Z voting power potentially enormous ... but you have to actually vote!

4. **Candidates nearly always have important differences.** Although you may think "All candidates are the same" or "I don't want to vote for the lesser of two bad candidates," candidates nearly always have substantial differences that can make a difference to you. These can be very obvious and clear differences, such as being pro-choice vs. anti-abortion, or they can be more subtle differences, such as in whether they view the U.S. as a terrible place in need of fixing or as a nation of great, hopeful people. Voting lets you clarify who you want representing you.

5. **Voting is a civic duty.** Many people worked hard for the right of all citizens to vote. Initially, only white male landowners over 21 were allowed to vote, and it took centuries for voting in the U.S. to be a right for all adult citizens, including women, individuals over 18, and people of color. Even if you don't feel like voting, vote on behalf of those who fought and died for your right to be able to vote.

6. **Voting is an opportunity for change.** Odds are there's something in your community you'd like to be different, from more bike lanes to lower taxes to more support for schools. Here's your chance!

7. **Voting directly affects your money.** Money and taxes are another way that candidates often differ. Do you pay taxes? Do you have student loans? Are you on your parents' or your employer's health insurance? Politicians make decisions about how money gets spent on these things – and how much you have to pay. If you want a say in how your taxes are spent, in how much student loans are subsidized or forgiven, or whether health insurance is a privilege or a right, you have to vote.

8. **Voting affects your life for years to come.** Candidates for office have different views on topics with longstanding implications,

such as climate change, education, civil rights, and health care. Some politicians are charged with appointing judges who have lifetime appointments and these judges can substantially impact those issues and others for a generation.

9. **Vote or don't complain.** If you don't vote, don't complain about what happens next. Whether the person you voted for wins or loses, your vote means you expressed your opinion, and it means you put your money where your mouth is.

**See also:** **Chapter 2:** What the Constitution Says about Voting
**Chapter 4:** Why Participating in Presidential Elections Matters
**Chapter 15:** How to Decide who to Vote for

# CHAPTER 2

# What the Constitution Says about Voting

Where does our right to vote come from? The U.S. Constitution. Come take a walk with us into our country's history to learn how voting came about and why it's so important.

1. **Creating our Democracy**. After the Revolutionary War earned our independence from Britain, our Founding Fathers officially ratified a new Constitution on June 21, 1788. The American Experiment of democracy was something the world had never seen before. Yes, the Ancient Greeks flirted with democracy and the Romans had a Senate, but in an era where the European powers were ruled either by emperors or kings, it was a monumental undertaking. Was it perfect? Of course not. But just the idea that George Washington would be elected into office and not try to seize power and become an emperor was something seriously incredible. It is monumental both that he willingly stepped down after two terms and that all candidates after him who lost a presidential election have willingly conceded and engaged in a peaceful transition. America is not perfect and our Founding Fathers were definitely not perfect either, but what was created starting in the late 1700s and continues today is truly a miracle. Our Constitution and our democracy requires all Americans to participate, defend it, and continue to make it better. Democracy dies when the people stop participating and stop believing in the system.

2. **How Democracies are Formed.** Throughout history, attempts to establish democracy often led to political instability, violence, and sometimes an even more authoritarian regime than before. Examples include the French Revolution, the Arab Spring, and Russia following the collapse of the Soviet Union. People in Belarus and Hong Kong are currently marching in the streets for democracy. The process of forming a democracy is often unpredictable and can provoke violent responses from those trying to undermine democracy. Yes, the United States has since experienced a civil war like many other nations have, and it has experienced times of civil unrest, including in the 1960s and 2020. But our system has always found a way to remain intact and move forward through the centuries in ways other countries and people around the world can only imagine. Voting is important in ensuring that this democracy continues into the future.

3. **"2 out of 3 Ain't Bad."** American voters determine who represents them in two of three branches of the federal government: the executive branch and legislative branch. Those branches determine who serves for a lifetime appointment as a federal judge in the third branch, the judiciary. While the system makes it difficult for voters to hold members of the judicial branch accountable, it helps ensure that judges do not make rulings based on public pressure or fear from being removed from their position by simply ruling on cases that go against what the other two branches desire.

4. **Fighting for Representation.** Although white men who owned property have always had the right to vote since the founding of this country, all other segments of the population had to fight for decades (women for over a century) to realize their right to vote.

5. **Civil War and the 13ᵗʰ, 14ᵗʰ, and 15ᵗʰ Amendments.** Following the Civil War, several amendments were adopted that abolished slavery and boosted voting rights. The Thirteenth Amendment

abolished slavery in the United States and made it impossible for Confederate states rejoining the Union to find a way to legalize slavery once again. The Fourteenth Amendment granted citizenship to any person "born or naturalized in the United States" and guaranteed equal protection under the laws of this country. The Fifteenth Amendment prohibited states from disenfranchising voters on the basis of "race, color, or previous condition of servitude."

6.  **Popular Election of Senators through the 17th Amendment.** Prior to ratification of the 17th Amendment in 1913, the American people did not directly vote for Senators, which made it difficult to hold them accountable.

7.  **Women's Suffrage through the 19th Amendment.** Women were given the right to vote in this country with the ratification of the 19th Amendment on August 18, 1920. Fun fact: Jeanette Rankin was the first woman elected to Congress – four years before women were officially given the right to vote.

8.  **Lowered voting age through the 26th Amendment.** Prior to the ratification of the 26th Amendment, 18-year-olds could be drafted into the Vietnam War but had no say in the political process that sent soldiers to Vietnam in the first place. Starting in 1971, people 18 years of age and older had the right to vote. What will you do with your vote?

**See also: Chapter 1:** Do you Know Why Your Vote Matters?
**Chapter 4:** Why Participating in Presidential Elections Matters
**Chapter 15:** How to Decide who to Vote for

# CHAPTER 3

# The Electoral College

The Electoral College has been a major player in presidential elections in the last few decades. It originally started as a compromise between Founding Fathers who thought presidents should be elected by popular vote and those who thought Congress should pick the president. How does it work and what are the implications for your vote? Read on...

1. **What is the Electoral College?** The Electoral College system calls for the creation, every four years, of a temporary group of electors equal to the total number of representatives in Congress. Technically these electors, not the American people, vote for the president. In modern elections, the first presidential candidate to get 270 of the 538 total electoral votes wins.

2. **Did the original Electoral College represent everyone?** Definitely not. When the electoral college was being created, there were disagreements about whether slaves could be counted in determining representation. Ultimately, the controversial "three-fifths compromise" established that black slaves would be counted as three-fifths of a person for the purpose of allocating representatives and electors and calculating federal taxes. The compromise ensured that Southern states would ratify the Constitution and gave Virginia, home to more than 200,000 slaves, 25% of the total electoral votes required to win the presidency. Women weren't even considered!

3. **Who decides how many electors each state gets?** It goes back to the census. The census determines how the 538 representatives

are allocated across states, and the electors are allocated equal to the number of representatives in Congress. For example, the State of New Jersey has fourteen electoral votes based on having two members in the Senate and twelve members in the House.

4. **The Electoral College: How It Works.** When a candidate wins the popular vote of a particular state, he or she receives a certain number of electoral votes, which is the same amount as the number of elected officials that state has serving in the House and Senate. States like Florida, which is a battleground state having a history of swinging back and forth in deciding which party to support. Other highly competitive states include Pennsylvania, Michigan, Wisconsin, Virginia, and Ohio with the winner of Ohio having won almost every presidential election since 1860.

5. **What is a faithless elector?** Electors are supposed to vote for the candidate who gets the popular vote in their state, but occasionally there are faithless electors who refuse to vote for the candidate whom their state had pledged to vote for. A 2020 Supreme Court ruling unanimously upheld laws that punish faithless electors.

6. **So can someone win the national popular vote and still lose the election?** Absolutely. This happened in 1824, 1876, 1888, 2000, and 2016, which has led to some people calling to abolish the Electoral College. In 2016, Hillary Clinton won the popular vote for President of the United States but lost the electoral college and as a result, did not win the presidential election. She only won 224 electoral votes, which is less than the 270 needed to secure victory.

7. **Your Vote Still Matters.** Even though the popular vote does not necessarily decide who wins a presidential election, that does not mean your vote does not matter. In fact, if 2016 taught the American people anything, it is that voting matters more than we realized. Around 138 million Americans voted in

2016, which was only about 58.1% of eligible voters with only 61.3% of voters participating in the hugely important state of Pennsylvania. When turnout is low and people choose not to exercise their right to vote, results like this where the popular vote and electoral college differ from one another are bound to happen.

**See also:** **Chapter 2:** What the Constitution Says about Voting
**Chapter 5:** Primaries Vs. Caucuses
**Chapter 11:** Funding Federal Elections

# CHAPTER 4

# Why Participating in Presidential Elections Matters

More people vote in presidential election years than in off years. Why is it important to take part in presidential elections? The President is the most powerful person in the country and is often referred to as the most powerful person in the world. Here are some ways your vote for President counts.

1. **Legislation.** After the House and Senate agree on bills, it's up to the President to either sign the bills or veto the bills, which gives Congress a chance to override the veto. The President can also employ a pocket veto, which occurs when the President does not sign a bill while Congress adjourns during a ten-day period. This type of veto makes it impossible for Congress to override.

2. **Lifetime Appointments to the Judicial Branch.** One of the reasons why presidential elections are so important is because this process includes determining who sits on the Supreme Court, which is the highest court in the land.

3. **Executive Orders.** Sometimes, the President bypasses Congress to sign an executive order, which generally have the force of law. Since they are not actually laws, however, the next President does not have to abide by those executive orders and can rescind them more easily than actual laws can be changed. There are limits

though. For example, President Obama bypassed Congress to create the Deferred Action for Childhood Arrivals (DACA) executive order, which allowed some individuals brought to the U.S. illegally as children to receive a renewable reprieve from deportation and become eligible for a work permit. President Trump rescinded the DACA executive order, but the Supreme Court recently ruled that the way the Trump Administration went about rescinding DACA was unconstitutional. It is likely that if Trump is re-elected, he will again attempt to rescind DACA in a way that would pass Supreme Court review.

4. **Cabinet Members.** With final approval from a Senate confirmation process, the President appoints individuals who serves in his or her cabinet as leaders of different government agencies. So when it comes to who serves as head of the Department of Defense during times of military conflict or head of the Department of Education when decisions are made regarding student loan guidance or protection from gender-based harassment, the people making those decisions are given the authority to do so by first being appointed to those positions by the President. For example, dangerous precedents have been established by the Department of Justice and Attorney General William Barr when it came to the prosecutions of Roger Stone and Michael Flynn, both of whom were indicted by Special Counsel Robert Mueller. Barr pushed for a lighter sentence on Stone even though he did not cooperate at any point with prosecutors and for the case against Flynn to be dropped even though he committed perjury.

5. **Armed forces.** The President is also the Commander-in-Chief of the Armed Forces. It is our responsibility as voters to ensure that anyone who becomes President values human life and respects the sacrifices made by members of the military, so as to not endanger military or civilian lives in senseless conflicts.

6. **Nuclear launch codes.** Last but certainly not least, the President also possesses the nuclear launch codes and has authority to

launch nuclear weapons for retaliatory or intentional first use. Although there is a detailed procedure for nuclear weapons launch, it is important for the public to have faith in a president who could initiate the use of nuclear weapons without apparent cause and to prevent the president from being pushed into making nuclear retaliatory decisions in haste.

**See also:** **Chapter 1:** Do you Know Why Your Vote Matters?
**Chapter 6:** Vote Down the Ballot and on all Ballots
**Chapter 15:** How to Decide who to Vote for

# CHAPTER 5

# Primaries vs Caucuses

Elections seem to last forever – it seems like as soon as one election ends, another campaign begins! The process actually includes primary elections or caucuses. Before candidates are chosen to represent the two major political parties in the United States in presidential elections, states hold primary elections, caucuses, or both to determine who secures the nomination.

1. **Party candidates are chosen by delegates at their convention.** The two major political parties (Democrats and Republicans) have conventions at which state delegates cast votes on behalf of their state for presidential candidates. These conventions are like big meetings at which candidates discuss the party's platform, which is the statement of what the party stands for. Delegates vote for candidates based on the results of their state's primary or caucus. For the first time in history, as will be discussed later in the book, the Republican Party chose not to have an official platform at their 2020 convention.

2. **Primary Elections.** A primary system is simple: voters vote for the person they want to represent each part. You might receive an "I voted" sticker and then whoever wins that states receives either a proportion or all the delegates that state awards.

3. **Open Primary.** In an open primary, any voter can appear and pick a candidate from any party meaning that registered

Republicans and registered Democrats can vote in the opposing party's primary.

4. **Closed Primary.** In a closed primary, voters can only participate in the primary election for the party they are registered for.

5. **Caucuses.** A caucus takes much longer than a primary because voters have to gather at a venue to hear out and discuss with supporters of different candidates. The more candidates there are, the more people there are to hear from and debate with. All 1,679 precincts in Iowa hold a caucus and venues can be anything from restaurants to high school gymnasiums. While Republican caucuses require just a secret vote to be held, Democrats move around a caucus site and supporters of different candidates move to different corners or areas of a room. Any candidate who receives less than 15% of the support of caucus attendees is not considered viable and that candidate's supporters must either choose a different candidate or remain uncommitted. A mathematical formula is used to determine how many delegates are awarded to candidates.

6. **Why is Iowa First?** Before 1907, parties selected all candidates through caucuses. Iowa switched to a primary system in 1916 before quickly switching back to a caucus in 1917. But it was not until 1972 that Iowa launched the presidential nomination process with the Democratic Party caucus starting that year and the Republican Party following suit four years later. Some say the change began after the chaotic Democratic Party Convention in 1968 during the height of the Vietnam War and that the party sought to make serious changes.

7. **Should Iowa be First?** Although there is no consensus about whether or not Iowa going first is fair, the complexity of the Iowa caucus has led some to believe that it should start the process early. Some say a more diverse state like Pennsylvania, Michigan, Ohio, or Colorado should begin the nomination process given how Iowa is not one of the more racially diverse states.

**See also:** **Chapter 2:** What the Constitution Says about Voting
**Chapter 11:** Funding Federal Elections
**Chapter 15:** How to Decide who to Vote for

# CHAPTER 6

# Vote Down the Ballot and on all Ballots

Voting for President is important, but there are lots of other decisions to make too!

1.  **State and Local Elections.** Non-presidential elections often see significantly lower turnout than presidential elections. For example, in 2014, only 36% of eligible voters participated in the election, which was the lowest turnout since 1942. During the 2008 and 2012 Presidential Elections, voter turnout in New Jersey was 73% percent and 67% respectively. But, the state governor elections in 2009 and 2013 saw significant drop in turnout with only 47% and 40% respectively.

2.  **Governor.** From signing bills into law to balancing the state budget to appointing judges to serve on state courts, determining who serves as governor is important for every state. Other responsibilities of the governor include making their state more attractive for businesses and managing property taxes. Just like the President appoints people to serve as heads of different federal departments and agencies, governors do the same in their states, which impacts statewide policies regarding issues such as public housing, the environment, responding to health pandemics like COVID-19, and more.

3.  **State Legislature.** State legislatures are the governing bodies that vote on and pass laws within their respective states just as

Congress does at the federal level. They can also override vetoes of any legislation a particular Governor refuses to sign and ensure that balanced budgets are passed each year. State district maps are not the same as congressional maps so two municipalities can be represented by the same state legislators but different federal legislators. As will be discussed in a later chapter, state legislatures determine how congressional maps are drawn, which can lead to gerrymandering, which is when boundaries are manipulated to favor one group over another. By voting and participating in these elections, it makes corrupt practices like gerrymandering much more difficult to occur because one of the effects of voting is more accountability.

4. **Sheriffs, District Attorneys, and Other Positions.** You might live in a district or municipality where you can vote for your sheriff or prosecuting attorneys. If you want more accountability for agencies such as police departments or feel that certain groups of people are unfairly treated by the law and justice system, vote for these positions if you have the opportunity to do so. Whenever a school budget is voted on and passed by local school boards, taxes are often impacted for those living in that particular school district. It's important to have a say in how much you pay in local taxes or how much your taxes might change on an annual basis.

5. **Initiatives.** From local school budgets to the recent trend in giving people the right to decide whether marijuana should be legalized, take advantage of opportunities when you have the chance to decide something for yourself rather than people voted into office who you might not feel best represents you and your beliefs.

**See also:** **Chapter 2:** What the Constitution Says about Voting
**Chapter 4:** Why Participating in Presidential Elections Matter
**Chapter 15:** How to Decide who to Vote for

PART 2

---

# Party Politics in the United States

# CHAPTER 7

# Development and Evolution of the Republican Party

Many voters who only vote based on their political party affiliation don't realize how much political parties change and evolve over time. The Republican party in 2020 is not the same as it was just a few decades ago. The Republican Party under Donald Trump is vastly different than it was under Dwight Eisenhower.

1. **Party of Lincoln.** The first Republican President of the United States was Abraham Lincoln, who led the nation during the Civil War and passed the 13th, 14th, and 15th Amendments. Given that the South that seceded from the Union following the election of Lincoln in 1860, it is safe to say that the Republican Party was not popular in the South. By 1896, Republican support in the South was essentially non-existent.

2. **Progressive Republicanism.** Republican President Theodore Roosevelt established the Food and Drug Administration and pushed antitrust measures to break up the monopolies that existed around the turn of the twentieth century. Republican President Dwight Eisenhower expanded social security when Richard Nixon was Vice-President. Republican President Richard Nixon created the Environmental Protection Agency and signed a series of environmental measures into law such

as the Endangered Species Act and the 1970 Clean Air Act. Since the 1980s, Republican Presidents like Ronald Reagan and Donald Trump have attempted to defund or annul the Environmental Protection Agency and programs like Social Security, especially as they both pursued deregulation and "trickle-down economics."

3. **First Women in Washington.** Republican Jeanette Rankin was the first woman elected to Congress in 1916 and Republican Margaret Chase Smith was the first woman to serve in both the House and Senate. Republican President Ronald Reagan appointed the first woman, Sandra Day O'Connor, to the Supreme Court.

4. **Republican-appointed judges.** Republican President Dwight Eisenhower appointed Earl Warren to serve as Chief Justice of the Supreme Court in 1953. Even though Eisenhower is not known as a champion or advocate for civil rights, his nomination of Warren to the court transformed American society with landmark rulings such as *Brown v. Board of Education* (granting equal educational rights regardless of race) and *Loving v. Virginia* (ruling that interracial marriage bans were illegal). Both President Dwight Eisenhower and later Democratic President John F. Kennedy respected the Supreme Court when it came to integrating schools and enforced the decision; however, more than twenty of President Donald J. Trump's federal judge nominees refused to say during their confirmation hearings whether they supported *Brown v. Board of Education.*

5. **Civil Rights.** Just as during the Civil War when it was the Republican Party that spearheaded the passage of the 13th, 14th, and 15th Amendments, Republican support in the House and Senate was crucial to overcome southern Democratic opposition to the 1964 Civil Rights Act. The only Republican Senator to oppose the Civil Rights Act was Barry Goldwater, who ran for President in 1964 and lost by a landslide.

6. **Southern Strategy and Transformation.** In 1968, in response to the 1964 Civil Rights Act, Republican President Richard Nixon launched the Southern Strategy, which was a strategy to increase political support among white voters in the South by appealing to racism against African Americans. The use of the Southern Strategy led to the South becoming a strong political base for the Republican Party. The party's use of identity politics surged to the point that the party eventually apologized in 2005 for using the strategy, although they continue to use racism to motivate their base to some extent.

7. **Immigration.** Republican President Ronald Reagan granted amnesty to millions of undocumented immigrants in the 1980s and Republican President George H.W. Bush established the lottery system for immigration that Republican President Donald Trump staunchly opposes.

8. **Reaganomics.** Beginning in the 1980s, and still being continued by President Trump, Republican economic policy has centered around reducing regulations, lowering corporate taxes and taxes for high-income earners, and reducing the "welfare state," which is the collections of grants, pensions, and programs the government runs to protect the health and well-being of its citizens, especially those in financial or social need. These "welfare state" programs include social security, public pensions, and government-supported health insurance.

9. **President Trump.** The Republican Party has not won the women's vote during a presidential election since 1988. Republican President Trump let the Violence Against Women Act expire, scaled back Title IX (which protects against discrimination based on sex in federally funded education such as public schools, first signed into law by Republican President Richard Nixon), and pushing defunding family planning (including birth control and Planned Parenthood, both of which were supported

by Republican President Richard Nixon), will probably not help Republicans win women voters in the foreseeable future.

10. **2020 Platform:** For the first time in its history, the Republican Party decided not to have an official platform at the convention where Trump was officially nominated to run for re-election. The official statement released said that the party will "continue to enthusiastically support the President's America-first agenda." No new platform will be unveiled until the 2024 Presidential Election but should Trump become re-elected, his political agenda would probably continue to consist of reforming entitlement programs such as Social Security, Medicare, and Medicaid, along with repealing the Affordable Care Act and enacting tougher immigration measures.

**See also:** **Chapter 4:** Why Participating in Presidential Elections Matters
**Chapter 8:** Development and Evolution of the Democratic Party
**Chapter 15:** How to Decide who to Vote for

# CHAPTER 8

# Development and Evolution of the Democratic Party

As mentioned, many voters who only vote based on their political party affiliation don't realize how much political parties change and evolve over time. The Democratic party in 2020 is not the same as it was just a few decades ago. The Democratic Party under President Barack Obama was vastly different than it was when the Dixiecrats ruled the party.

1. **Origins of the Democratic Party:** The Democratic Party can trace its origins back to the election of Andrew Jackson as President in 1828. Jackson was a slave owner from Tennessee, and he pushed for removal of Native American tribes from their ancestral lands, culminating in the Trail of Tears during his administration. As voting rights slowly expanded to include white males who did not own property, Jackson's victory began the Democratic Party's domination of federal politics up to the eventual election of Republican Abraham Lincoln and the Civil War.

2. **Southern Support for Democrats.** During the era between the American Civil War and the signing of the Civil Rights Act in 1964, the Democratic Party received strong support from the South during presidential elections. The Republican Party

had some support early on after the Civil War as Black suffrage expanded. But by 1896, Black representation in southern state legislatures and the number of African Americans representing southern states in Washington were almost non-existent and led to the Republican Party having a minimal presence in the South. The Republican Party was not interested in protecting its base of southern voters who were primarily African American.

3. **Dixiecrats.** Although it was considered an upset in 2017 when Doug Jones was elected to serve as Democratic Alabama Senator and people are surprised how close elections now are between Republicans and Democrats in Texas, 100+ years ago that would have been business as usual for Democrats. Famous southern Democrats, or Dixiecrats as they were often referred to, included Huey Long, Ross Barnett, George Wallace, Strom Thurmond, Lester Maddox, and Jesse Helms. While defending segregation in Alabama, Democratic Governor George Wallace gave his famous "Segregation Now, Segregation Forever" speech. When it comes to civil rights for African Americans, it is clear that the Democratic Party has a dark history in many respects.

4. **Changing Party Platform.** While the Democratic Party at one time embraced right wing conservatism, which made it especially popular in the South, that began to change with the election of Franklin Roosevelt in 1932 and the New Deal that created programs such as Social Security and unemployment benefits. Progressivism moved further into the party when President Lyndon Johnson signed the 1964 Civil Rights Act, the 1965 Voting Rights Act, and enacted Medicare and Medicaid. The party would later elect President Barack Obama as the first ever African American president in 2008 and continue to take a more liberal approach on social issues like LGBT rights.

5. **2020 Platform**: At the Democratic convention where Joe Biden was officially nominated to be the candidate for President, the party released a 50 page platform that stated the goals of

reforming the immigration and criminal justice systems, achieving universal health care through a public option, making college more affordable and more accessible, and raising minimum wage so that it reaches $15 per hour by 2026. Climate change and environmental justice are also heavily addressed but there is no mention of a "Green New Deal" as some of the more progressive members of the Democratic Party have previously called for. The platform can be found at democrats.org.

**See also:** **Chapter 4:** Why Participating in Presidential Elections Matters
**Chapter 7:** Development and Evolution of the Republican Party
**Chapter 15:** How to Decide who to Vote for

# CHAPTER 9

# "Throwing Away Your Vote?" The Struggle for Third Parties in the United States

To run as a third-party candidate in any election in the United States is extremely difficult. Third-party candidates are often perceived as being the reason Republicans or Democrats lose a close election when more than two candidates are on the ballot. Because of that reputation and their inability to fundraise and compete with the major party candidates, some argue that voting for a third-party candidate is the equivalent of "throwing away your vote." But is that the case? Is it better for American citizens to vote for major party candidates even if they do not believe in their ideas and agenda fully, or should it be considered acceptable to vote for candidates who probably have no chance in winning the election but who citizens may agree with more on issues? Even if third-party candidates have no chance of winning, have they in the past impacted who has won elections, particularly a presidential election?

1. **Dominance of Major Political Parties:** There has never been a candidate from a third-party ever elected president with the most successful candidate being Theodore Roosevelt when he ran as a progressive in 1912 and won 88 delegates in the Electoral College. The last third-party candidate to ever win any electoral

votes was George Wallace in 1968, having won five southern states that awarded him 46 electoral votes. Wallace won 13.5% of the popular vote but only 9% of available electoral votes.

2. **Electoral College:** All but two states award all of their state's electoral vote to the candidate who wins the popular vote outright, which means third-party candidates have to win states entirely to receive any electoral votes towards the Electoral College. Not being able to split the electoral votes by proportion of the popular vote of a particular state won makes it very challenging for third-party candidates to remain competitive. That is why Ross Perot won 19% of the popular vote in 1992, which was the largest share of the popular vote won by a third-party candidate since 1992, but was awarded zero electoral votes.

3. **How Americans Identify:** According to a Gallup poll conducted in July and August 2020, 41% of the American electorate identified themselves as Independents with 31% labeling themselves as Democrats and 26% as Republicans. That poll is conducted every two or three weeks and while the percentage of Independents is usually either in the thirties or forties, it never crossed 50%. Once the Independents who lean towards one party or the other are eliminated, the number of true Independents is usually just under or just over 10%. Gallup stated that 88% of Americans identify with either the Republican Party or Democratic Party, although the Pew Research Center believes it can be as high as 92%.

4. **Why vote?** For Millennial and Generation Z voters who may be discouraged or feel uncomfortable having to choose between two political parties, do not sacrifice your beliefs and convictions and always strive to be the change you wish to see. That starts with voting and from there either change the major political parties to your liking or find a party and candidate that will listen to your vision for America.

**See also:** **Chapter 4:** Why Participating in Presidential Elections Matters
**Chapter 7:** Development and Evolution of the Republican Party
**Chapter 8:** Development and Evolution of the Democratic Party

# CHAPTER 10

# Efforts to Keep you from Voting

The U.S. was founded on democratic ideals, including the right for citizens to vote for who will represent them in government. So why would anyone try to keep people from voting? Well, unfortunately there's a long history of voter suppression in the U.S. Some of those efforts continue today. It's important be alert and aware so you can protect your right to vote. The herculean efforts to suppress young voters are proof that the participation of youth in democracy is valuable.

1. **Voter suppression as American as apple pie.** Throughout history, both Democrats and Republicans have a history of mobilizing and suppressing voters to their advantage. During the late nineteenth century, southern states dominated by the Democratic Party that wanted to make it more difficult for African Americans to vote began adopting poll taxes, education requirements, literacy tests, and grandfather clauses (that allowed people to vote only if their grandfather had voted, disenfranchising newly-freed slaves whose grandfathers were not eligible to vote). In addition, Joe Rich, who served as head of the Voting Section for the Bush Administration's Department of Justice from 2000 to 2004, clarified "The GOP agenda is to make it harder to vote. You purge voters. You don't register voters. You pick the states where you go after Democrats." Yikes.

2. **1965 Voting Rights Act.** During the civil rights movement in

the 1960s, the 1965 Voting Rights Act was signed into law. It required states and jurisdictions with reprehensible records of voting discrimination and repression to seek approval from either the Department of Justice or a federal judge in Washington before it could change any of its voting laws. A formula was used to determine which states and jurisdictions needed to first seek approval; many of those areas happened to be in the South.

3. **... but the Voting Rights Act was gutted in 2013.** In a five-to-four 2013 decision in *Shelby County v. Holder*, the Supreme Court stated that because suppression tactics like poll taxes and literacy tests were made illegal, and minority voter registration was much higher than it was in the 1960s, the formula was no longer needed, essentially destroying the Voting Rights Act. All five judges who ruled in the majority were appointed by Republican presidents. As a result, Alabama, Arizona, Alaska, Georgia, Louisiana, Mississippi, Texas, South Carolina, and Virginia no longer need to seek federal approval before changing any election laws. Many of those states and jurisdictions of other states have since enacted measures that rolled back early voting, purged voter registration lists, and enacted voter ID laws.

4. **Requiring ID to vote.** Requiring voter identification effectively suppresses the votes of youth and the poor. In Georgia in 2005, Georgia Governor Sonny Perdue signed a bill that required voters to present photo identification when voting; the list of universities with "acceptable" identification excluded private historically black colleges such as Morehouse College, private all-female colleges such as Agnes Scott College and Spelman College, and Georgia Institute of Technology (Georgia Tech), a major public university with thousands of students. In Wisconsin in 2011, shortly after being sworn in as Governor of Wisconsin, Governor Scott Walker signed an act requiring identification to be shown at polling places and to place an absentee vote; only 10 of the 36 public and private universities in Wisconsin, however, offered identification cards that met the requirements. In 2011,

Alabama enacted voter ID legislation, then closed 31 DMV offices that could issue valid identification cards, including DMVs in 8 of the top 10 counties with non-white voters. Other states, including Virginia and North Carolina, passed similar voter ID laws, suppressing the vote of hundreds of thousands of voters, often young, minority, students, or poor.

5. **Requiring felons to resolve all court fees to be eligible to vote.** On July 16, 2020, the Supreme Court allowed Florida to continue barring convicted felons from voting until they paid all court fines and fees despite the fact that in 2018, voters in Florida chose to amend the Constitution and end the disenfranchisement of people convicted of felonies "upon completion of all terms of sentence, including parole and probation," with the exceptions being murder and rape convictions.

6. **Gerrymandering.** Redistricting of congressional districts occurs every ten years following the census and it is conducted by each state's legislature. When state legislatures redraw congressional maps for partisan purposes and use the process to benefit one political party at the expense of another, that is when redistricting becomes gerrymandering, which is illegal. Proving in a court of law that a state legislature engaged in gerrymandering is not always easy; what makes gerrymandering important now is its impact on young voters and how it severely marginalizes them and make it much more difficult for them to be properly represented. In addition to its voter ID laws to suppress young voter turnout, North Carolina has also attempted to make young people's vote meaningless by the way congressional maps have been drawn. North Carolina's creative district drawing has led to only three of its 13 seats in the House of Representatives (23%) being held by Democrats, despite Democrats being 36% of the state's registered voters. The majority Republican-appointed Supreme Court has indicated unwillingness to enforce laws against gerrymandering: In June 2018, the Supreme Court overruled lower federal courts and disagreed with their assessments that Texas

had discriminated on the basis of race when it drew certain congressional and state-level districts. In 2019, the Supreme Court ruled that federal courts have no jurisdiction and are powerless when it comes to hearing cases seeking to challenge perceived partisan gerrymandering, and in October 2019, the Supreme Court rejected challenges made to Ohio congressional districts drawn by the Republican-controlled state legislature. Similar challenges made in Michigan were also put on hold by the Supreme Court.

7. **Claims of voter fraud to enact more stringent voting requirements.** Despite repeated accusations of voter fraud, none has been substantiated. According to a study conducted by Loyola University, over one billion votes were cast in elections between 2000 and 2014. Among all those ballots, researchers could find only thirty-one potential instances of people pretending to be someone else when voting and acknowledged that the actual number could even be lower. The study was published by the *Washington Post* and is cited in the Further Reading section at the end of this book. The Brennan Center for Justice investigated speculation about voter fraud in Wisconsin during the 2004 presidential election and found one case of voter impersonation due to poll workers' clerical error; two alleged cases of fictitious voting were not verified. In South Carolina, state Attorney General Alan Wilson claimed that more than 900 deceased people had ballots cast with their name in 2010. After an investigation was conducted, however, only five votes were left unexplained with many of those five voters having the same name as their deceased parents or having their records mixed up at the Department of Motor Vehicles.

8. **Not extending deadline for voting during the COVID-19 pandemic.** On April 6, 2020, the Supreme Court refused to extend the deadline for absentee voting by six days for Wisconsin with its primary election that was the next day even with the Coronavirus pandemic. The two sides arguing before

the Supreme Court were the Republican National Committee and the Democratic National Committee with the more conservative judges siding with the Republicans and more liberal judges siding with the Democrats. It came down to whether the court believed a federal judge had the right to unilaterally change the absentee voting procedures for a particular state days before an election. The Supreme Court declared that federal judges did not have the right to do so, regardless of the public health emergency.

9. **Not allowing absentee voting during the COVID-19 pandemic.** In May 2020, in response to the COVID-19 pandemic, a Texas ruled that "any eligible Texas voter who seeks to vote by mail in order to avoid transmission of Covid-19 can apply for, receive and cast an absentee ballot in upcoming elections during the pendency of pandemic circumstances." Usually the only exceptions in Texas to allowing people to vote by other means besides in-person are for people away from home, in jail, with disabilities, and those over the age of sixty-five. However, the U.S. Court of Appeals for the Fifth Circuit strongly disagreed with Judge Biery and stated his ruling, "will be remembered more for audacity than legal reasoning" and the Supreme Court sided with the appeals court. In a state like Texas that is considered to be highly competitive between Donald Trump and Joe Biden, access to mail-in ballots could be a deciding factor in who wins the state and its 38 electoral votes.

10. **What does this mean for Millennials and Generation Z voters?** It means pay attention and vote! Millennials and Generation Z are the youngest and most diverse generations currently in the United States. These two generations also have a smaller percentage of white voters than previous generations. Among Millennials, 20% are Hispanic/Latino and 59% are white, compared to Baby Boomers, who are 10% Hispanic/Latino and 73% white. Generation Z is even more ethnically and racially diverse. Despite these efforts to suppress votes of young people,

students, poor, and non-white individuals, a lower proportion of Millennials voted in 2016 compared to Baby Boomers. If all eligible Millennials and Generation Z voters voted, they would outnumber Baby Boomers!

**See also:** **Chapter 1:** Do you Know Why your Vote Matters?
**Chapter 11:** Funding Federal Elections
**Chapter 12:** Super PACs and Dark Money

# PART 3

# Who Funds U.S. Elections and Why

# CHAPTER 11

# Funding Federal Elections

Elections cost money. An enormous part of campaigning is fundraising and any campaign that struggles with fundraising cannot survive in the long run. How elections are funded in the U.S. leads many people to consider the extent to which donors influence elections. Let's dig in.

1. **Why does money matter?** Public disclosure was long central to political candidates' fundraising, with the idea that full disclosure and transparency will increase trust in candidates and reduce the potential for corruption. Public disclosure has been a foundational, sustainable, and controversial part of the political system.

2. **How much money are we talking about?** In 2016, Democratic presidential candidate Hillary Clinton's campaign raised $1.4 billion; Republican presidential candidate Donald Trump's campaign raised $957.6 million. In 2016, the total amount of money spent on the presidential election and congressional elections was $6.5 billion.

3. **How can candidates raise funds?** Presidential candidates can raise funds by asking for donations to their own campaign or by asking for donations to their party's apparatus (e.g., the Republican or Democratic National Committees), which can fundraise on behalf of the party and give money to specific candidates in their party. Candidates also can receive some matching

federal funds if they meet certain fundraising and public support requirements. Foreign money is not allowed to fund campaigns under any circumstances. And then there are the political action committees (PACs), and Super PACs.

4. **What are PACs?** PACs are tax exempt organizations that pool campaign contributions from members and donate those funds to campaigns for or against candidates, ballot initiatives, or legislation. Political federal multi-candidate PACs may contribute to candidates in these ways: $5,000 to a candidate or candidate committee for each election (primary and general elections count as separate elections); $15,000 to a political party per year; and $5,000 to another PAC per year.

5. **In addition, PACs may make unlimited expenditures that are to neither a candidate nor political party.** Some PACs are affiliated with one political party, such as Democratic Governors Association or Americans for Conservative Solutions (affiliated with the Republican Party). Others represent interests such as agribusiness, the energy sector, Wall Street, gun rights, health care, pharmaceutical industry, and more.

6. **What are Super PACs?** Briefly, Super PACs are organizations that allow individuals to donate unlimited amounts of money to political action committees with certain restrictions. Super PACs are so important, we devoted a whole chapter to them. See *Chapter 10: Super PACs & Dark Money*.

7. **How money influences politics.** What is absolutely essential to our democracy is maintaining the independence of the judicial branch. Increasing money spent on elections of politicians in the executive (president) and legislative (senators and representatives) branches of government can greatly impact who gets nominated to the bench. No money is ever given to Super PACs or campaigns directly without expecting something in return. For example, when the National Rifle Association spends millions of dollars during election cycles, they are expecting the

nomination of judges who will block gun control efforts. When Goldman Sachs or any of the major Wall Street institutions make political contributions, they would like to see judges who would like to scale back or eliminate the 2010 Dodd-Frank Wall Street Reform and Consumer Protection Act, which placed strict regulations on lenders and banks in an effort to protect consumers and prevent another economic recession. When judges are forced to make such major decisions even on other issues like abortion access, LGBT rights, or access to voting, it should be on the merits of the Constitution and not whether or not they owe favors to large political donors of the politicians who appointed them as federal judge. For young people questioning whether or not voting is worth it, the best way to ensure the integrity and independence of the judiciary is to vote.

8. **So how are corporations funding elections?** In 2016, corporations that contributed to presidential elections included: Goldman Sachs ($6.3 million), Exxon Mobil ($2.8 million), and JPMorgan Chase and Company ($2.7 million).

9. **So why vote?** Given how much money it costs to run for office and how much money dominates politics, it might be discouraging or seem pointless to exercise your right to vote. You might think that politicians are only going to listen to who fills their campaign coffers. But if people voted in large numbers, this money has a much less significant impact because when it is all said and done, the ballot box tallies votes, not money.

**See also: Chapter 4:** Why Participating in Presidential Elections Matters
**Chapter 10:** Efforts to Keep you From Voting
**Chapter 12:** Super PACs and Dark Money

# CHAPTER 12

# Super PACs & Dark Money

As mentioned in chapter 9, Super PACs are really important but also struggle with transparency with donors being able to remain anonymous.

1. **What are Super PACs?** Super PACs are organizations that can raise an unlimited amount of money in order to support or defeat political candidates with the money coming from individuals, corporations, and other outside groups.

2. **Why is this important?** To understand Super PACs, we have to understand *Citizens United v. Federal Election Commission*. Prior to the 2010 *Citizens United* ruling, both corporations and unions were banned from spending money of their own to influence federal elections because of the unfair advantage they would be perceived to have. In the 2010 *Citizens United* case, the Supreme Court stated that corporations and unions have the same constitutional rights as citizens when it came to free speech, and that since money is one exercise of free speech, corporations and unions could spend from their general treasury funds on "electioneering communication." The only grounds that free speech (donations) could be limited was *quid pro quo* corruption (when someone specifically indicates "I will give you x to do y."). The *Citizens United* decision paved the way for Super PACs, which allow individuals to donate unlimited amounts of money to political action committees as long as the money went

to independent expenditures with the committees monitoring the independent expenditures being Super PACs.

3. **PAC vs Super PAC.** Regular PACs cannot receive more than $5,000 from a single individual and can only donate a percentage of the money to individual candidates. Super PACs have no limits to how much money can be raised but can neither donate directly to campaigns nor coordinate with them. The guidance around "not coordinating" is ridiculously inadequate. Super PACs designed to support a specific candidate are often established by former staffers and aides like the Restore Our Future Super PAC that was established for Mitt Romney when he ran for President by former campaign staffers. In efforts to raise awareness about Super PACs and how much money – and how few rules — they actually have, comedian Stephen Colbert formed a Super PAC in 2011 that raised over $1 million.

4. **Dark money.** Another important aspect of Super PACs is "dark money," which refers to spending to influence political outcomes without disclosing the source of the money. Politically active nonprofits such as 501(c)(4)s, opaque nonprofits, and shell companies may give unlimited amounts of money to super PACs without disclosing their donors. Although Super PACs are legally required to disclose their donors, some of these groups are effectively dark money outlets when the bulk of their funding cannot be traced back to the original donor.

5. **Relationship with candidates.** Although political candidates are not allowed to coordinate with Super PACs, political candidates can be featured as speakers at fundraising events for Super PACs as long as unlimited contributions are not solicited. Instead, limited contributions up to five thousand dollars are allowed.

6. **Inclusive or exclusive?** During the first half of 2011, liberal Super PACs raised $7.61 million with more than 80% of the funds coming from 23 donors and for conservative Super PACs,

$17.61 million was raised with more than 80% of the money coming from 35 donors. Some have argued that having so few donors contribute so much to Super PACs is a sign of the increasing prevalence of income inequality in the United States infusing itself into politics.

7. **Why vote?** For young voters who find these numbers discouraging, vote for the candidates you desire. Then Super PACs and dark money will both become much less significant.

**See also: Chapter 4:** Why Participating in Presidential Elections Matters
**Chapter 10:** Efforts to Keep you From Voting
**Chapter 11:** Funding Federal Elections

# PART 4

## The Vote Itself

# CHAPTER 13

# Registering to Vote and Voting by Mail

It's so important to register to vote and plan how you're going to ensure your vote is counted. This section describes how to get started.

1. **Registering to Vote.** You have to actively register to vote in the location where you live. You will be asked if you want to register for a particular party affiliation (Democrat, Republican, Independent), which could affect which primaries and caucuses you can vote in. Thanks to the 1993 National Voter Registration Act, states are required to allow registration by mail, the Department of Motor Vehicles, and at certain state offices (like those for public assistance and disability).

2. **When can I register to vote?** Some states allow you to register as soon as you turn seventeen or within six months of your eighteenth birthday. In Michigan, you also have to be a legal resident in your city or municipality for at least thirty days by Election Day. Different states have different deadlines for registering to vote. Although you can register early, you have to be at least 18 years old on election day to be able to cast a vote.

3. **What is required to register to vote?** States have different rules about who can register to vote and how registration can happen. For example, in California you have to be a U.S. citizen, resident of California, at least eighteen years old by Election Day, and

not in state or federal prison or on parole. You also cannot be declared mentally incompetent by a court of law.

4.  **Can I register to vote online?** Most states have online voter registration, Maine, New Hampshire, New Jersey, North Carolina, Mississippi, Arkansas, Texas, North Dakota, South Dakota, Montana, and Wyoming have yet to implement any kind of online voter registration legislation. If you live in a state that has been aggressively purging voter rolls and removing registered voters for whatever reason, make sure you are still registered early enough so that way you have time between now and Election Day to re-register yourself in time to vote.

5.  **What are my options for voting?** States allow voting in person, by mail (including absentee ballots), or both. With the current COVID-19 pandemic, it's important to pay attention to changes your states are making related to voting by mail and what the courts are ruling constitutional or unconstitutional. See below for options in your state.

6.  **Voting Early.** If you're voting in person, some states allow early voting for individuals who may have difficulty making it to a polling place and waiting in line on Election Day. These states offer no early in-person voting, which means you must vote on Election Day unless the state allows voting by mail or absentee ballots: Alabama, Connecticut, Kentucky, Mississippi, Missouri, New Hampshire, Pennsylvania, Rhode Island, and South Carolina offer no early in-person voting. When it comes to being able to vote by mail, pay attention to changes your states are making and what the courts are ruling are constitutional or unconstitutional.

7.  **Voting by Mail.** These states automatically mail ballots to all eligible voters: Washington, Oregon, California, Utah, Colorado, Vermont, Hawaii, New Jersey, and the District of Columbia. Other states allow you to request an absentee ballot "no questions asked," and others have specific requirements for requesting

an absentee ballot (See below). If you are voting by mail, also pay attention to whether your state allows ballots to be counted only if they are received by Election Day, or if they are postmarked by Election Day but received afterwards.

8. **Absentee ballots.** States usually allow individuals to request an absentee ballot when they will not be able to go in person to vote on election day. With the current COVID-19 pandemic, these rules around absentee ballots are changing as states work to expand or restrict voting. Check your state's requirements to ensure up-to-date information. As of printing September 2020,

   a. Nine states are automatically mailing every registered voter an application to receive an absentee ballot: Connecticut, Delaware, Illinois, Iowa, Maryland, Massachusetts, New Mexico, Ohio, and Wisconsin.

   b. Three states require no specific justification to approve an absentee ballot request: Delaware, Massachusetts, and Missouri.

   c. Seven states allow voters to cite COVID-19 as sufficient justification for voting absentee: Alabama, Arkansas, Connecticut, Kentucky, New Hampshire, New York, and West Virginia.

   d. Six states indicated that concerns about COVID-19 alone are not a sufficient justification for requesting an absentee ballot; these states require additional justification beyond COVID-19: Indiana, Louisiana, Mississippi, South Carolina, Tennessee, Texas.

9. **Getting your ballot delivered so your vote is counted.** If you're voting by mail/absentee ballot, it's important to submit your ballot as soon as you know who you are voting for to give yourself the best chance for your ballot to count. Some states have ballot drop boxes if you do not want to use the mail.

**10. Why is it so complicated?** States are allowed to set their own rules re: voting. As discussed previously, some states have histories of voter suppression, including young, minority, and poor voters. Don't let the rules discourage you – make sure you register and vote!

**See also: Chapter 4:** Why Participating in Presidential Elections Matters
**Chapter 14:** From Waiting in Line to Inside the Voting Booth
**Chapter 15:** How to Decide who to Vote for

# CHAPTER 14

---

# From Waiting in Line to Inside the Voting Booth

As we write this, there's a pandemic of COVID-19, which means that many more people will be voting by mail than usual. If you are voting in person, here's what to expect.

1. **Confirm your voter registration, voting location, and voting hours.** Usually this information is sent to you after you register to vote. There are also websites for your county, city, or state to confirm you are registered and to look up your voting location and hours. It's important to go to the correct location where you registered so you can be checked off the list and your vote can be counted correctly. Some states are expanding the opportunity to allow voting at any voter location, but check first!

2. **If you have any special needs, contact your voting office to ensure accommodation.** Special needs include mobility issues, such as not being able to stand or needing a wheelchair ramp; visual difficulties to where you might not be able to see the ballot clearly; you require an aide or service animal to accompany you; or anything else. Remember that the right to have accommodations for your disabilities are rights that were clarified through voting.

3. **Pick your time to vote.** Some people like to be early birds,

others go mid-day, and still others will stop by the voting location after work. Be aware that there may be delays getting set up in the morning, and the polls might not open exactly on time or be ready when they open. Also be aware that states vary on who is allowed to cast votes after polls close. California, for example, requires that everyone in line when the polls are closed is allowed to cast their vote, but individuals who show up after the polls are officially closed are not allowed to vote. Given delays, it makes sense to go early, just in case.

4. **Expect to stand in line for a while.** Bring whatever you need to make the wait comfortable, including appropriate clothing/jacket/umbrella, water and snacks, and your phone/music. Standing in line can also be a great opportunity to meet your neighbors!

5. **Get checked in.** Once you reach the front of the line, poll workers will check you in by matching your name against their voter lists. In many places, these are still stacks of paper with names and addresses listed alphabetically. Whether you need to show identification varies by state. Generally, it is a good idea to bring your ID and something that shows your address, such as a utility bill, just in case.

6. **What do I do if my name isn't on the voter list?** Even if your name is not on the voter list at the polling location, you generally have the right to vote with a provisional ballot. Your provisional ballot will be counted only after the elections official has confirmed you are a registered voter and you did not vote anywhere else in that election. The poll worker can give you information about how to check if your provisional ballot was counted and, if it was not counted, the reason why. Be aware that sometimes elections are called before provisional ballots are counted.

7. **After you are checked in, you may vote by paper ballot.** In many places, you are handed a *paper ballot* on a large piece of paper inside a large envelope or folder. Paper ballots usually have

vertical columns for each position, listing each candidate below, and vertical columns for initiatives, indicating your options. You may be led or directed to a voting booth where you have privacy by a curtain or other barrier. Usually only one person is allowed at the booth, except for children or required aides. You can mark your vote with a pen or pencil in the booth, then carry your completed ballot inside its envelope or folder to either hand to a poll worker or drop into a container or enter it into a voting machine. Make sure to check out with the poll workers before you leave to make sure your vote was fully processed.

8. **After you are checked in, you may vote by electronic ballot.** For electronic ballots, there is usually a touch screen or a screen like an ATM where you indicate your votes. You are then asked to confirm your votes and a receipt may be printed. Make sure to check out with the poll workers before you leave to make sure your vote was fully processed.

9. **Get a sticker!** Many polling places offer an "I voted!" sticker that you can proudly wear to demonstrate you completed your civic duty.

**See also:** **Chapter 4:** Why Participating in Presidential Elections Matters
**Chapter 10:** Efforts to Keep you from Voting
**Chapter 13:** Registering to Vote and Voting by Mail

# CHAPTER 15

# How to Decide Who to Vote For

Voting and participating in the democratic process can become very difficult if you do not know which candidate to vote for. As a result, you can find yourself susceptible to psychological tactics used to influence your vote such as where the names of candidates are placed on the ballot. Informing yourself and understanding how the candidates feel about issues that matter to you is a crucial step in helping you make the most informed decisions possible on Election Day.

1. **Discover the issues that matter most to you.** In order to figure out which candidates or political party to support during an election, you need to discover within yourself the issues that mean most to you. Not everyone is going to agree on which issues are most important. For example, an August 2020 Pew Research survey of issues voters viewed as very important found voters identified the economy (79% endorsed), health care (68%), a Supreme Court appointment (64%), the coronavirus pandemic (62%) and gun policy (55%) as very important. Seeing these issues as important does not mean they have the same perspectives on how to address the issue. Other issues that you could potentially find important include foreign policy, immigration, climate change, and more; your stance on issues such as these will shape your ideology and help you choose between candidates.

2.  **Research where candidates stand on those issues.** Although there is a chance that a candidate might align 100% with how you feel on every issue, you have to be prepared for the possibility of picking the candidate who most aligns with you on the issues you believe matter most. In a nation that has hundreds of millions of registered voters, it is impossible for candidates to make everyone completely satisfied even among supporters. It is your responsibility, however, to make the most informed decision you can; that starts with researching the positions taken by candidates and platforms established by the major political parties. The candidates have websites that state their positions on different issues and help give you an idea of what a term in office of theirs would look like for the country. Whether someone is challenging an incumbent like Joe Biden is challenging Donald Trump in 2020, or like in 2008 when neither Barack Obama nor John McCain were the incumbent, listening to their speeches, researching their positions and priorities online, and keeping track of who is contributing funding to the different campaigns are all things that you can do leading up to Election Day.

3.  **Making tough decisions.** Once you've learned everything you can about the candidates, it's time to make choices. This is where your clarity on where you stand on issues is really important. Some people choose to vote party line (all Democrat or all Republican) because the party views generally line up with their perspectives; this doesn't always work though, such as in primaries. You also can choose what issues are more important to you (e.g., a candidate's stance on gun control vs. civil rights, or abortion vs. climate change). You can look at the funding to the campaigns, to judge for yourself if you have concerns about who is funding the candidates. Finally, you can also look at evidence of the candidate's character. Does the candidate pledge to represent all constituents or only those who vote for them? Is the candidate professional or unprofessional? Would you feel proud to have the candidate represent you? Remember, you likely won't

get exactly what you want, but make the best choice based on how you balance what is important to you.

4. **Ballot Placement:** One tactic that could impact who people decide to vote for, especially for those either unsure or uninformed while submitting their ballot, is where the names of the candidates are placed on the ballot. People are often drawn to what catches their eye first. Studies have shown that the candidate listed first receives up to 2.5% boost over those listed afterwards; this effect is increased when political parties aren't listed, races were not highly publicized, and no incumbent is running. Some states now vary candidate order across precincts to reduce bias. The less you know about yourself as a voter and the less you know about the candidates, the more likely you are tobe influenced by the placement of the candidates' names. Ideally you can do your homework and make your decisions before looking at the ballot so you can be confident in your choices.

See also: **Chapter 1:** Do you Know why your Vote Matters?
**Chapter 4:** Why Participating in Presidential Elections Matters
**Chapter 6:** Vote Down the Ballot and on All Ballots

PART 5

# How You Can Protect Your Voting Rights and Stay Informed

# CHAPTER 16

# Social Media Giving People a Voice: For Better or Worse

With the rise of social media, people are able to express themselves and connect with others around the world like never before in history. Political candidates and elected officials are constantly using platforms like Twitter to communicate with their constituents and establishing Facebook and Instagram pages for people to follow. But beware: people can very easily spread misinformation even if it is unintentional and can try and appear to their followers as an expert in politics with little to no consequences.

1. **Fake News.** Leading up to the 2018 midterm elections, it was pushed by many in the news media and on social media that caravans of disease-ridden migrants were coming up from Mexico and entering the United States. None of that was true, but when members of the news media with huge followings push narratives — true or untrue — they can spread like wildfire. One of the most important things you can do as a young voter with the opportunity to participate in this democracy for decades to come is to be as smart and informed as you possibly can. You do not have to be an expert on everything, but there are plenty of ways to pay attention and staying involved without succumbing to fake news and any kind of propaganda meant to deceive you.

2. **Misinformation.** Misinformation, particularly on social media, can come in two forms. First, whether it is through trolls or foreign adversaries attempting to subvert American democracy, anyone can post something on social media that is misleading and dishonest. Even if Facebook and Twitter eventually remove the post or put a warning label next to it, millions of people can potentially see it and think it is true. Statements or videos that distort reality, such as when a doctored video of Nancy Pelosi falsely portrayed her as slurring while speaking, create enormous damage by purposely manipulating voters. The other issue is while it is great that social media gives people a chance to express themselves, it also gives people the idea that they are experts on subjects they have no business posting about or discussing with thousands and maybe even millions of followers. Not everything you read on the Internet that already fits a narrative and belief you might possess is accurate. This also leads to people spreading misinformation without even realizing it and being used as what some have referred to as "useful idiots." One of the most effective ways for American adversaries to spread misinformation is to have Americans unwittingly do it for them.

3. **Foreign Interference on the Internet.** According to the Mueller Report, during the 2016 Presidential Election, a Russian organization called the Internet Research Agency purchased over 3,500 advertisements on Facebook worth over $100,000. Within the last ten weeks of the election, 3,814 Internet Research Agency accounts on Twitter tweeted 175,993 times. The organization was headquartered in St. Petersburg, Russia and headed by Vladimir Putin's associate Yevgeny Prigozhin. It's important for voters to understand how foreign interference works and to avoid it; read the Mueller Report between now and Election Day, especially as more of it becomes unredacted over the coming weeks and months.

4. **Social Media Misleading Voters.** When you see an account on Facebook, Twitter, or Instagram, or a group for you to join on

Facebook that you think is with people of similar political interest, or a meme or video of something that catches your eye and is telling you what you want to hear, just remember that you may really not have any idea who exactly you are engaging with and where money might be coming from to fund those kinds of misinformation operations.

**See also:** **Chapter 1:** Do you Know why your Vote Matters?
**Chapter 11:** Funding Federal Elections
**Chapter 12:** Super PACs and Dark Money

# CHAPTER 17

# Apps and Voting

Before you get too excited, there's no current app that will allow both an anonymous vote (protecting against voter coercion, suppression, or vote selling) and an auditable vote (to protect against any errors or breaches because recounts can be conducted). There are some small scale tests of voting-by-app for some overseas voters or those with disabilities, and there are also apps that simplify the process of registering to vote, finding your polling location, and informing you about the elections happening in the different districts your municipality is located in. For young voters especially, these apps can be very useful.

1. **Register to Vote.** As of now, if you live in California, Pennsylvania, Missouri, Arizona, Colorado, and Massachusetts, you can scan your license and become a registered voter within seconds.

2. **Vote.org.** You can check if you are a registered voter, which is extremely important if you live in a state where voter rolls are attempted to be purged. Absentee ballots can also be requested if you do not plan on voting in person and users of the apps can also check on the voter id requirements of each state should they exist.

3. **TurboVote.** This app sends text and email reminders to vote the day before an election is happening where you are eligible to vote.

4. **Voatz** is an app that proposes to allow voting through your smartphone but has yet only been pilot tested in small

communities. Cybersecurity experts, however, say it's not secure, with the potential for adversaries controlling the election or loss of privacy outweighing the convenience.

5. **VoteSaveAmerica.com/states.** This website provides in-depth information for every state such as the number of electoral votes each state contributes in the electoral college, the latest updates announced by a state's respective governor regarding the voting process, which is important with the ongoing pandemic, and key dates like voter registration deadline, when in-person absentee voting can occur, deadline to request a mail-in ballot and the date recommended to submit that ballot by to ensure it counts on Election Day. You can register to vote through the site and the date of Election Day is also provided.

6. **Vote411.org.** Vote411 allows anyone to type in their home address and see who and what will be on their specific ballot, along with providing information about upcoming special elections. It also provides a link to your state's agency that oversees voting, which should allow you to check and make sure you are still a registered voter who has not been purged from the voter rolls.

7. **Ballotpedia.org.** One thing this website does is allow people to type their home address to see a sample ballot including all the candidates and resolutions. For example, in fall 2020, the State of New Jersey not only has the presidential election, but it also has three ballot measures that focus on marijuana legalization, property tax deductions for peacetime veterans, and delaying redistricting. So rather than wait until Election Day to see those resolutions and potentially vote on something you are not edu-cated about, this website gives voters a chance to be much more informed. You can also sign up for a newsletter and receive all the information you need concerning things like early voting and voter id requirements.

8. **Aclu.org.** The American Civil Liberties Union has webpages for each of the 50 states that provide voting information, along

with a phone number of theirs you can call if there are any irregularities at your polling location and the phone number for each state's Division of Elections or equivalent agency.

**See also:** **Chapter 1:** Do you Know why your Vote Matters?
**Chapter 4:** Why Participating in Presidential Elections Matters
**Chapter 6:** Vote Down the Ballot and on All Ballots

# CONCLUSION

Millennials and Generation Z voters will have many opportunities to not only vote in presidential elections, but to shape the future of their country and determine what it will look like for years and decades to come. Everything in this book that might seem discouraging such as the Electoral College, Super PACs, and dark money will not matter nearly as much if young voters truly flexed their muscles.

Our democracy is special.

Our democracy is worth defending.

Our democracy is worth your participation.

# FOR FURTHER READING

Aberbach, Joel D. & Gillian Peele. (2011). *Crisis of Conservatism: The Republican Party, the Conservative Movement, & American Politics after Bush*. Oxford University Press: New York.

Amar, Akhil Reed. (2005). *America's Constitution: A Biography*. Random House, Inc.: New York.

Fisher, Patrick. (2014). *Demographic Gaps in American Political Behavior*. Westview Press: Colorado.

Gaskins, Keesha & Sundeep Iyler. (2012). The Challenge of Obtaining Voter Identification. *Brennan Center for Justice*. http://www.brennancenter.org/sites/default/files/legacy/Democracy/VRE/Challenge_of_Obtaining_Voter_ID.pdf

Key, V. (1955). A Theory of Critical Elections. *The Journal of Politics, 17*(1), 3-18. Retrieved from http://www.jstor.org/stable/2126401

Levitt, Justin. (2007). The Truth About Voter Fraud. *Brennan Center for Justice*. https://www.brennancenter.org/sites/default/files/legacy/The%20Truth%20About%20Voter%20Fraud.pdf

Levitt, Justin. (2014, Aug. 6). A comprehensive investigation of voter impersonation finds 31 credible incidents out of one billion ballots cast. *Washington Post.* https://www.washingtonpost.com/news/wonk/wp/2014/08/06/a-comprehensive-investigation-of-voter-impersonation-finds-31-credible-incidents-out-of-one-billion-ballots-cast/

Panagopoulos, C. (2009). Campaign Dynamics in Battleground and Nonbattleground States. *The Public Opinion Quarterly, 73*(1), 119-129. Retrieved from http://www.jstor.org/stable/25548065

Piven, Frances Fox & Lorraine C. Minnite & Margaret Groarke. (2009). *Keeping the Black Vote Down: Race and the Demobilization of Voters.* The New Press: New York.

Piven, Frances Fox & Richard A. Cloward. (1988). *Why Americans Don't Vote.* Pantheon Books: New York.

The Center for Information & Research on Civic Learning and Engagement. (2015). State-by State Map of Youth Voter Turnout, Voter Registration, and Youth Demographics. http://civicyouth.org/maps/elections/

The Center for Information & Research on Civic Learning and Engagement. (2012, Nov. 7). *At Least 80 Electoral Votes Depended on Youth.* http://civicyouth.org/at-least-80-electoral-votes-depended-on-youth/

Tisch, Jonathan M. (2016). Young Voters in the 2016 General Election: Data and Analysis of Youth Turnout, Vote Choice, and Composition of Electorate. *The Center for Information & Research on Civic Learning & Engagement.* http://civicyouth.org/wp-content/uploads/2016/11/CIRCLE-Full-Exit-Poll-Analysis_Final.pdf

# ACKNOWLEDGEMENTS

Voting is a community event, and so was writing this book. We have been overwhelmed with the positive responses we received from so many people eager to ensure young people vote. We wish to thank the following for their expert and insightful comments: Casey Adams, Marc & Dianne Beilinson, Lourdes Blanco, Walt Dawson, Mark Del Rosario, Remi Farnan, Jennifer Felner, Alison Feuer, Shaun Hettinger, Amy Hess, Chris Kelleher, Hilary Westgate, and Thai Wood. We appreciate Diego G. Diaz for cover design and photography, Deana Riddle at Bookstarter and Jerry Dorris at AuthorSupport.com for interior design and publishing support, Jacqlyn Burnett for public affairs, and Cassandra Blake for exemplary administrative assistance.

## JEREMY LEVINE:

What I found fascinating about this book idea of Dr. Jennifer Wisdom is how closely it related to my master's thesis about young voters being demobilized. It has been a great experience working with Dr. Wisdom, especially on a subject I had previously researched extensively and find both very interesting and very important. The 2020 Presidential Election is one of the most important elections in American history and I am proud to have been part of this effort to inspire young Americans to participate in the democratic process and flex their political muscle. I wish to thank Dr. Wartyna Davis, Dean of the College of Humanities and Social Sciences at William Paterson University, for recommending me to work on this project. I have always admired her work both in higher education and as a Councilwoman in Bloomfield,

NJ so to have her think of me to work on this book is truly an honor. Most importantly, I want to say thank you to my mother for taking me to libraries as a kid going as far back as "Mommy and Me" and teaching me about the importance and magic of reading. There will never be enough words to describe the impact she has had in my life.

## JENNIFER WISDOM:

I am honored, humbled, and delighted to be the recipient of such amazing support from friends and colleagues. Thank you especially to: Katrina Amaro, Tara Amato, Lourdes Blanco, Diego G. Diaz, Jennifer Felner, Prea Gulati, Kristina Hallett, Sunny Istar Lee, Mary Mitchell, Billy Monks, Linda Warnasch, Valerie Weaver, and Laura Zorich. And of course, many thanks to my daring, adventurous, and efficient co-author, Jeremy Levine, without whom this book would not exist. He is a superstar.

# ABOUT THE AUTHORS

**Jeremy Levine**, MA, is an Adjunct Professor at multiple universities in New Jersey and New York who teaches in a variety of areas including political science, sociology, economics, business, and math. He has a Bachelors in Finance from Fairleigh Dickinson University and a Masters in Public Policy in International Affairs from William Paterson University. His teaching career began in 2017 and has included universities such as NYU, The College of New Jersey, Pace University, and for the W.E.B. Du Bois Scholars Institute at Princeton University. Jeremy also lectures and guest speaks on highly sensitive political topics like the Mueller Investigation, the rise of Vladimir Putin, Erik Prince and the use of private mercenaries in modern warfare, the Syrian Civil War, and the resurgence of white nationalism in the United States.

**Jennifer Wisdom**, PhD MPH, is a former academician who is now an author, consultant, speaker, and principal of Wisdom Consulting. As a consultant, she helps curious, motivated, and mission-driven professionals to achieve their highest potential by identifying goals and then providing them with the roadmap and guidance to get there. Jennifer created the best-selling *Millennials' Guides* series. The first book, *Millennials' Guide to Work*, helps Millennials and others achieve success and respect at work. The second book, *Millennials' Guide to Management & Leadership*, helps Millennials be successful and impactful managers and leaders. Dr. Wisdom is a licensed clinical psychologist. She has worked with complex health care, government, and educational environments for 25 years, including serving in the

U.S. military, working with non-profit service delivery programs, and as faculty in higher education. She is an intrepid adventurer based in New York City and Portland, Oregon. She can be reached at www. leadwithwisdom.com.

Made in the USA
Middletown, DE
08 July 2022

—

68814116R10050